KS2 HISTORY IS EASY
VIKINGS

THE
REVISION
SERIES

www.How2Become.com

As part of this product you have also received FREE access to online tests that will help you to pass History (The Vikings) for KS1 and KS2.

To gain access, simply go to:

www.MyEducationalTests.co.uk

Get more products
for passing any test at:

www.How2Become.com

Orders: Please contact How2Become Ltd, Suite 1, 60 Churchill Square Business Centre, Kings Hill, Kent ME19 4YU.

You can order through Amazon.co.uk under ISBN: 978-1911259121, via the website www.How2Become.com or through Gardners.com.

ISBN: 9781911259121

First published in 2017 by How2Become Ltd.

Typeset for How2Become Ltd by Anton Pshinka.

Disclaimer

Every effort has been made to ensure that the information contained within this guide is accurate at the time of publication. How2Become Ltd is not responsible for anyone failing any part of any selection process as a result of the information contained within this guide. How2Become Ltd and their authors cannot accept any responsibility for any errors or omissions within this guide, however caused. No responsibility for loss or damage occasioned by any person acting, or refraining from action, as a result of the material in this publication can be accepted by How2Become Ltd.

The information within this guide does not represent the views of any third-party service or organisation.

CONTENTS

THE NEW NATIONAL CURRICULUM

(Guidance for Parents)

WHY CHILDREN ARE TAUGHT HISTORY IN SCHOOLS

History is part of the primary syllabus. Studying history gives children an introduction to the major events which have shaped Britain, and provides them with a better understanding of historical global relations. The aim of the subject is to inspire a deeper curiosity for how society has changed over the course of time.

WHAT ARE THE AIMS OF THE HISTORY SYLLABUS?

The syllabus provides children with:

- An understanding of British history as a chronological narrative, from ancient times to the present day. It focuses on how British people have been influenced by the rest of the world, and how they have made their own influence felt.

- An understanding of the essential events and features of the history of the world as a whole, focusing on the earliest civilisations, most powerful empires, and the ways in which humanity has succeeded and failed.

- A wide historical vocabulary and an understanding of key terms and concepts such as 'civilisation' and 'society'.

- An introduction to wider historical concepts such as: continuity and change, cause and consequence, similarity, difference, and significance; and how to use them to make connections, draw contrasts, analyse trends, frame historically valid questions, and create their own structured accounts, including written narratives and analysis.

- An understanding of the importance of evidence when putting forward historical opinions. This also includes thinking about why some people interpret events or facts differently.

- An introduction to historical perspective, by considering contexts such as location, economics, politics, religion, and key points in time.

Key Stage 1

Below we have outlined specific criteria that should be considered when studying History at Key Stage 1.

Pupils should:

- Develop an awareness of the past, using common words and phrases to describe the passage of time.

- Know where the people and events they study fit within a chronological framework, and identify similarities and differences between ways of life in different periods.

- Use a wide vocabulary of everyday historical terms.

- Ask and answer questions, choosing and using parts of stories and other sources to show that they know and understand key features of events.

- Understand some of the ways in which we find out about the past, and identify different ways in which it is represented.

Key focuses

- Changes in national life within living memory.

- Historical events beyond living memory, with national and/or international significance.

- The lives of individuals who have contributed significant achievements.

Key Stage 2

Below we have outlined specific criteria that should be considered when studying History at Key Stage 2.

Pupils should:

- Continue to develop a chronologically secure knowledge and understanding of local, British, and world history.
- Establish clear narratives within and across the studied historical periods.
- Note connections, contrasts, and trends over time and develop the appropriate use of historical terms.
- Address questions about change, cause, similarity, difference, and significance.
- Construct informed responses that involve thoughtful selection and organisation of relevant historical information.
- Understand how our knowledge of the past is constructed from a range of sources.

Key focuses

- Changes in Britain from the Stone Age to the Iron Age.
- The Roman Empire and its impact on Britain.
- Britain's settlement by Anglo-Saxons and Scots.
- The Viking and Anglo-Saxon struggle for the Kingdom of England, up to the time of Edward the Confessor.
- A local history study (this will of course vary from school to school.)
- A study of an aspect or theme in British history that extends pupils' chronological knowledge beyond 1066. (E.g. the changing power of monarchs – using case studies such as John, Anne, and Victoria.)
- The achievements of the earliest civilisations, such as Ancient Egypt or Ancient China.
- Ancient Greece, its achievements, and its influence on the western world.
- A non-European society that provides contrasts with British history, such as early Islamic civilisation, or the Mayan civilisation

INTRODUCTION
TO THE
VIKINGS

INTRODUCTION TO THE VIKINGS

The Vikings were a civilisation of warriors and invaders who specialised in naval attacks – they were very good at building ships and navigating the sea. They came from Scandinavia (the area where we now find Denmark, Norway, and Sweden).

Through their many raids and attacks on the rest of Europe from these places, the Vikings had a huge impact on society. They were active from about the year 800 to the year 1066, just under 1,000 years ago.

Look at the headings in each of the thought bubbles below – these will form the sub-headings throughout this first chapter.

Thinking about these topics will give you an insight into the world of Vikings, and help you understand the chapters that will come later.

Join our Viking, Torvald, as he introduces you to his people!

MEET THE VIKINGS

The Vikings have become notorious figures in world history for their legendary ruthlessness and brutality when it came to invading foreign lands. However, it is important to note that this is not all they did – they were also traders and builders.

More peaceful Scandinavians came to settle in Britain due to the warmer climate and fertile farmland, mixing with the Anglo-Saxons who lived in Britain during this time. These Vikings brought their own style of construction to Britain, and were excellent craftsmen. They travelled the seas to Britain either to find somewhere to live, or to find goods to buy to bring back to their homes.

Ornate Viking wood carving of a wolf

However, it is much more interesting to read about the pillaging pirates that were the aggressive Vikings! These travellers were much less friendly; they were warriors, who sought glory, fame, and fortune.

Viking warriors travelled in huge boats called longships, which at the time were the most impressive ships humans had ever created. They came to Britain and Ireland to steal and kill – the word 'Viking' may actually mean 'invader' or 'raider' in Old Norse, the language of the Scandinavians at this time.

These bandits ransacked monasteries, stealing jewels and gold from defenceless monks! The Vikings and the Anglo-Saxons did not share the same religion, meaning that the northern invaders did not care that the monasteries were sacred places for the people they were 'visiting'.

Eventually, the Vikings were able to go beyond random raids and take some British land under control. More on that later!

QUESTION 1

On the map below, draw a circle around the area that we can refer to as Scandinavia.

QUESTION 2

Draw your own image of a Viking wood carving below! Think about including detailed patterns and animals.

ANSWERS

QUESTION 1

QUESTION 2

This question has no wrong answers – show your creativity!

VIKING BELIEFS AND RELIGION

Before we talk too much about what the Vikings did abroad (and they did a lot!) it is important to be aware of who they were as a people in their own land. In other words, you should know what they thought was important and what they believed, in order to help you understand what may have driven them to plunder overseas as often as they did.

Why do you think the Vikings travelled so much?

Although the Vikings shared a similar language to the Anglo-Saxons of Britain, their religions were hugely different. While the Britons had adopted Christianity, the Vikings were pagans who worshipped many gods and goddesses, and believed that the world in which humans and animals lived was just one of nine! See below for a summary of some of their most important gods.

NORSE GODS AND GODDESSES

Odin: The father of all gods. Odin was said to have endless wisdom, and was a god of poetry, art, and magic. However, he is a complicated figure: Odin also represented war, and often set people against each other in battle for his own amusement. He rode an 8-legged horse called Sleipnir (*the one who slides*).

Thor: A more straightforward, noble god. Thor was the thunder god, who wielded an unstoppable hammer called Lightning. This god protected the human world from giants and monsters, and helped the humans grow crops and be healthy.

Loki: The trickster and 'evil' god, culprit of many crimes against gods and humans alike. Loki could shapeshift, an ability he used in his schemes and murder plots against others. He sometimes did these bad things just to make himself laugh.

Hel: The giantess ruler of Helheim, or Norse hell. Hel was Loki's daughter, and was charged with looking after those condemned to the underworld. She was said to look like one half of her face was dead, and the other side was alive. Hel was capable of bringing plague and death to whole towns.

THE NINE WORLDS

Norse mythology tells us that Vikings believed that existence was cast between 9 worlds, which were found on the branches and roots of a vast, magical tree called Yggdrasil *(IGG-DRUH-SILL)*. The worlds were connected by rainbow paths, which the gods/goddesses could use to travel the universe. Other mythical creatures, such as giants (who were not really 'giant' – they were godlike devourers) and elves could also use these paths, which they often did when attacking each other.

These are the 9 worlds, as found in Yggdrasil:

- **Midgard** *(MID-GARD)*: the realm of humans.

- **Asgard** *(AZ-GARD)*: the realm of the Aesir tribe of gods and goddesses (such as Odin and Thor), where Valhalla is found.

- **Vanaheim** *(VAN-A-HAYM)*: the realm of the Vanir tribe of gods and goddesses (such as Njord – the sea god and Freya – the love god).

- **Jotunheim** *(YO-TUHN-HAYM)*: The realm of giants.

- **Niflheim** *(NI-VUHL-HAYM)*: The mist realm, home to ice creatures.

- **Muspelheim** *(MOO-SPUHL-HAYM)*: The fire realm, home to fire creatures.

- **Alfheim** *(ALV-HAYM)*: The elf realm.

- **Svartalfheim** *(SVA-TUHLV-HAYM)*: The dwarf realm.

- **Helheim** *(HELL-HAYM)*: The realm of the dead, where Hel is in charge.

VIKING BELIEFS

As well as being huge believers in myth and legend, the Vikings had many other personal and collective beliefs that were extremely important to them.

Perhaps the most important of these beliefs was to do with war and death. In the hearts and minds of Viking warriors, it was absolutely **vital** that they died a hero's death – cowardice was simply **not an option**. It is impossible to overstate the importance of this idea – a Viking's ultimate dream was to die with honour in battle.

> **Can you understand why Vikings dreamt of a hero's death?**

This strange-sounding dream is all to do with how Vikings hoped to spend **eternity** after they died.

If a Viking died with honour and bravery, then they would ascend to Valhalla *(VAL-HAL-UH)* (a great hall in Asgard) to live forever in bliss with the gods. Odin's Valkyries *(VAL-KUH-REEZ)* (spirit helpers) would pick up those deserving and fly them to Valhalla.

In Valhalla, the fallen heroes would drink and eat as much as they wanted. They would also fight each other for fun! It was where a Viking wanted to be, so they did all they could to fight bravely in the hope they would be rewarded with a pleasant afterlife.

On the other hand, Norse soldiers who did not fight bravely were said to end up in Helheim with Hel herself. Here, they would live in freezing temperatures forever – it was impossible to leave. What makes it worse, is that it was not only cowardly soldiers who were condemned to Helheim, but also those who died from disease or old age.

In other words, it was sometimes not enough to fight bravely to get into Valhalla. You actually had to be killed in battle in order to get a seat at Odin's table – surviving war meant being sent to hell when you eventually did die!

QUESTION 1

In the boxes on the left are the differing religions of the Vikings and Anglo-Saxons. In the boxes on the right are descriptions of these religions. By drawing a line between them, match both religions to their most accurate description.

Christianity	A belief in many gods, as well as many mythical creatures
Paganism	A belief in one god, including a faith in Jesus Christ.

QUESTION 2

In the box below, write down which of the Norse gods mentioned above (**Odin**, **Thor**, **Loki** and **Hel**) you find most interesting.

In the space below, write down a reason for your choice.

_____

_____

_____

_____

QUESTION 3

Complete the following crossword about the eight worlds of Yggdrasil.

ACROSS

4. Where the Aesir gods live, including Odin.

6. The world of the elves.

7. The Viking underworld, governed by Hel.

8. The home of fire creatures.

DOWN

1. The world where the dwarves live.

2. The giant realm, home to the mythical devourers.

3. The home of the Vanir tribe of gods.

5. A frozen and misty realm where ice creatures live.

QUESTION 4

Why it was so important for Vikings to fight bravely in battle.

ANSWERS

QUESTION 1

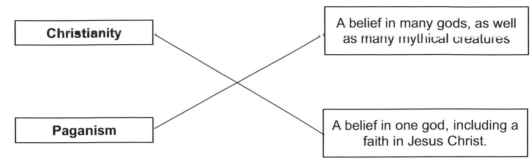

| Christianity | A belief in many gods, as well as many mythical creatures |
| Paganism | A belief in one god, including a faith in Jesus Christ. |

QUESTION 2

This question is based on personal opinion, but see below for an example response.

Odin

I find Odin to be the most interesting god, for a few reasons. Firstly, the fact that he was father of all gods suggests that he is the most powerful. I also enjoy how he is neither a god of pure good or a god of pure evil. Finally, I would also be interested to see what Sleipnir would look like in real life!

QUESTION 3

ACROSS

4. Where the Aesir gods live, including Odin: **Asgard**

6. The world of the elves: **Alfheim**

7. The Viking underworld, governed by Hel: **Helheim**

8. The home of fire creatures: **Muspelheim**

DOWN

1. The world where the dwarves live: **Svartalfhelm**

2. The giant realm, home to the mythical devourers: **Jotunheim**

3. The home of the Vanir tribe of gods: **Vanaheim**

5. A frozen and misty realm where ice creatures live: **Niflheim**

QUESTION 4

The reason it was so important for Vikings to fight bravely in battle:

- So they would go to Valhalla when they died.

VIKING SOCIETY (AND JUSTICE SYSTEM)

While these religious and mythological beliefs were an extremely important part of Viking society, there was more to Viking society that needs to be considered.

STORIES AND RUNES

Vikings were great storytellers. Not only did these stories often involve their gods and mythology, but also family, and tales of travel and war. The stories were mostly told orally (using the spoken word), with poems and epic tales being performed in public on a regular basis.

However, the Vikings did have an alphabet, made up of 'runes', which they used to write things down. People carved these runes into rock, to speak of their love for a family member, to give thanks to a god, or just to write down stories. Here is the Old Norse alphabet:

a b c d e f g h ij k l m n o p q r s t uvw x y z

"Using the Old Norse alphabet, write your name in the box below!"

EVERYDAY LIFE FOR A VIKING

As in most, if not all, of societies at the time (the year 800-1066), Viking society was male-dominated. Women mostly had to carry out domestic chores, such as looking after babies, cooking, and making clothes. Viking clothes took a very long time to make, as it all had to be done by hand. This clothing also had to be extremely warm – the Scandinavian weather could be brutally cold!

Male Vikings worked as farmers and builders, including making weapons as blacksmiths. Vikings were amazing craftsmen!

Of course, men were quite often away on raids, fishing, or travelling around looking to trade. In which case, the women had to take over the men's work, as well as carrying on with theirs!

Despite this, you could argue that Viking women had more rights and power than many other women in the world at this time. Divorce was allowed, and it was not acceptable for a man to use violence against his wife: if he did so, he could face punishment from the rest of the community. More on the Viking legal system later!

Can you imagine being a child during the time of the Vikings?

Children's lives were also tough! They didn't go to school or have classes – they simply had to follow their parents and learn the trades and tasks they would have to take over when they grew up. Basically, children learned to chip in with hard work from as early an age as possible.

VIKING HOMES

Whether a family lived in a small farming village, or an isolated farm of their own, all its members would share one space in a building called a **longhouse**. Most Viking longhouses were narrow, made out of wood, and had thatched rooves. One end of the longhouse would be used to keep a workbench and tools, while the other was used to house the farm animals! Animals had to live inside most of the time, due to the freezing winters and chilly springs and autumns.

Viking families used the central spaces of these houses for a large fire, which they used as a light source and to cook food. Also, Vikings put benches in this area, where they could sit and socialise as a break from work. This central area was also where they put their beds. During mealtimes, meat, fish, and vegetables would be left to cook on the fire, while family members gathered to chat and tell stories.

All in all, these Viking longhouses were bustling, warm, and homely places where families could spend time together, relax, and work.

VIKING JUSTICE SYSTEM

The Vikings had official systems of government and law, which they took very seriously. Eventually, when kings rose to power, these laws were officially adopted by kingdoms and countries.

Early Vikings, however, did not write any laws down! Instead, each community had a 'Lawspeaker', who would have to learn and remember every single law created without writing them down, and say them aloud when needed!

This was clearly important and difficult work, so these speakers were usually well-respected and wise members of the community, who everyone trusted to be fair and knowledgeable.

How do you think the Vikings punished criminals?

All free men in a community would gather together and decide on a set of laws – they would agree on what would be acceptable in their village and what would not be. Vikings outlawed things such as theft and violence against women. The Lawspeaker would then learn and remember what was decided, and use this knowledge to assist in trials if someone was accused.

Those who were found guilty by the community would either be fined or 'outlawed'. Being 'outlawed' was a terrifying prospect for a Viking, as it meant that they were shunned by the rest of their community. An outlaw would have his possessions taken, and no one was allowed to help him; he was no longer welcome in the community.

This meant that an outlaw had to leave their village and attempt to settle somewhere else. To make it worse, outlaw status meant that your enemies had the freedom to hunt you down and kill you, and not face any punishment!

For less clear-cut cases, such as in disputes over land, the community would sometimes allow the quarrelling parties to settle their dispute by fighting with swords and shields! The loser of these duels was said to be the person whose blood touched the ground first, but they would often result in death. The result of such a fight had to be respected, as it was said that the gods would reveal the rightful winner of a dispute this way.

The Vikings called this process 'Holmgang' *(HOLL-M-GANG)*, **which had strict rules**

QUESTION 1

Using the Old Norse alphabet (shown below), translate the message shown in the box below into English. Write your answer in the lines underneath.

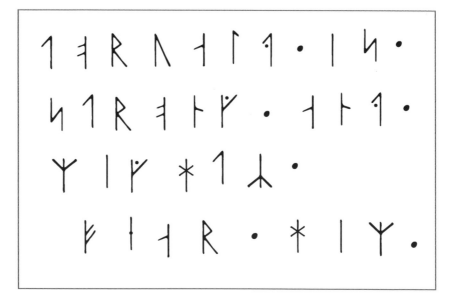

QUESTION 2

Imagine you are a child living during the Viking era. Write a short diary entry for one day in which you had to help your mother with her tasks in the morning, and then help your father with his tasks in the afternoon.

These tasks could include sewing, carving wood, working with metal, building, farming, hunting, fishing and even raiding and trading!

Dear Diary,

QUESTION 3

Sketch a plan of a Viking longhouse. Show and label all the rooms and furniture!

QUESTION 4

Imagine you are a Viking who has just been outlawed. Write a little bit about how you would feel and what you would do.

_____

_____

_____

_____

_____

ANSWERS

QUESTION 1

The message reads:

> # TORVALD IS STRONG AND MIGHTY
> # FEAR HIM

QUESTION 2

*This question is based on creative writing, but see below for an example response.

Dear Diary,

Today was another hard day. After getting up early, I set to work with Mother at the loom to make clothes – we must be able to wrap up warm when winter comes again. I am still learning how to sew, so my main role today was to be a good assistant. Later, I was sent out to look for firewood we could burn to help cook our food – a very important job.

Although this meant that my morning's work was complete, my father still expected me to report to him for an afternoon shift. My father is a talented blacksmith, and he expects me to follow in his footsteps. So, I must watch him work and learn from him every day. I enjoy learning this craft, although it involves lots of heavy lifting and being scarily close to fire! I shall sleep well tonight,

Until tomorrow, Diary,

Torvald.

QUESTION 3

Your drawing should look something like this:

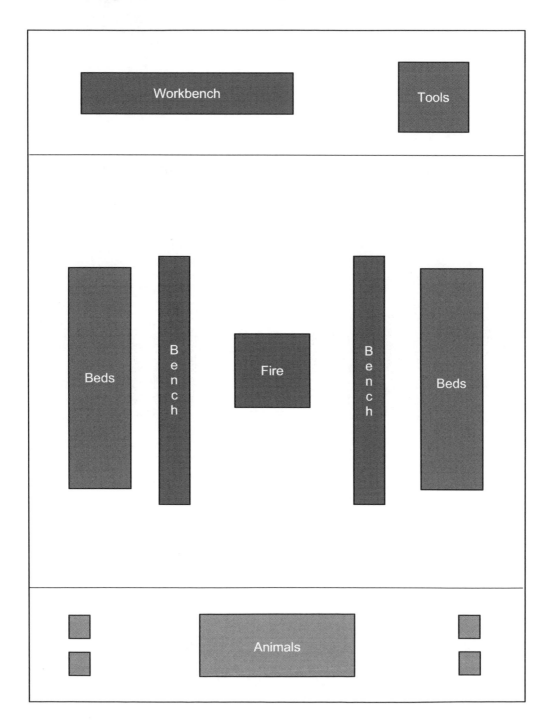

QUESTION 4

This question is based on creative writing, but see below for an example response.

It has been one week since I was made an outlaw by the rest of my tribe. I have been forced to trek far away from my home and family – otherwise my life and those of my family would have been in danger.

I am lonely, cold, and hungry. I have no possessions anymore. This is a scary time for me. I plan to settle down in a nearby village. I hope they will accept me.

I wish I had not done what I did.

HOW ARE YOU GETTING ON?

VIKING WARRIORS AND THEIR LONGSHIPS

Now we have talked about what the Vikings did while at home, let's look at how they managed to be so successful abroad! What did the Vikings need to own and have to do in order to be good raiders? In short, they were incredibly tough, and had simple but effective equipment, which they were experts in using.

VIKING WEAPONS AND EQUIPMENT

Viking helmets were made from iron, and many provided protection for the eyes and nose. Most did not actually have horns!

Viking battle-axes were very light, and very sharp. The long shaft allowed the warrior to strike from distance. The axe blade was often decorated with gold or silver.

Viking shields were big and round, and made of wood. Vikings often decorated their shields with intricate patterns, family crests or mythological figures.

In addition to the equipment shown above, raiding Vikings would wear leather shoes and armour. However, only the richest and most powerful Vikings would have swords, as they were the only ones who could afford to buy anything with such a large amount of iron.

VIKING LONGSHIPS

As we have talked about, Vikings were the masters of sea travel. They were extremely comfortable on the water, using ships for travel, to fish, and to attack.

The most famous of their ships were the Viking longships, which were sometimes called dragon-ships, named after the wooden figureheads some chose to install on the front of their ships. These figureheads were probably added to scare enemies and to mark themselves out. They were also said to ward off sea monsters!

The ships themselves would be between 20 and 30 metres long, and able to hold between 40 and 60 men. Despite their size, the Vikings tried to make the ships as light as possible, so they could move them around quickly when they landed. This also meant that they could get off and onto them as fast as possible, to make surprise attacks as easy as possible!

Fjord *(FYOORD)*: a river-like channel carved into land by ice.

Another important feature of the longships was that they were flat-bottomed – their undersides did not plunge deep into the ocean. This meant that they could sail in very shallow water, such as the Scandinavian fjords and the Anglo-Saxon's rivers. Think about how useful it was for the Vikings to be able to sail across the sea and all the way down a river, right into the heart of an opponent's city!

A Viking Longship

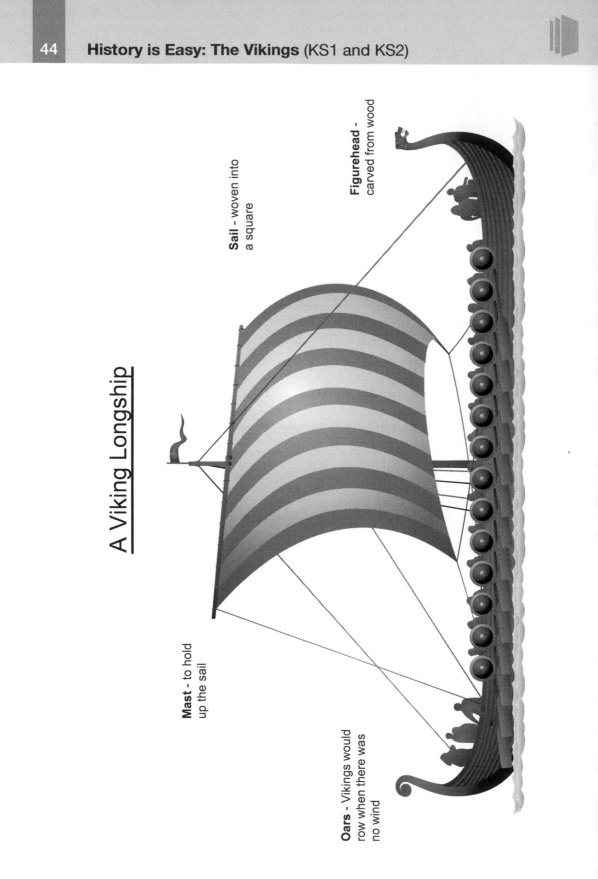

Sail - woven into a square

Figurehead - carved from wood

Mast - to hold up the sail

Oars - Vikings would row when there was no wind

Question Time!

QUESTION 1

In the space below, make your own design for a Viking shield! Consider using an intricate pattern and/or mythological creature in your drawing.

QUESTION 2

Why do you think that Vikings liked to decorate their shields, and adorn their weapons with gold and silver? Think about topics discussed in the 'VIKING BELIEFS' section (page 21).

_____

_____

_____

_____

QUESTION 3

Imagine you are an Anglo-Saxon who lives in a town or city on the banks of a river. Write a little bit about how you might feel if you saw a Viking longship charge down your river into the heart of your city!

_____

_____

_____

_____

ANSWERS

QUESTION 1

This question has no wrong answers – show your creativity!

QUESTION 2

Your answer should read something like this:

Vikings decorated their shields and weapons because they were very important to them. For a Viking, nothing was more important than dying a hero's death in battle. So, Vikings were very proud of the weapons that allowed them to do this. Adorning their weapons with gold and silver was one way of showing this.

QUESTION 3

This question is based on creative writing, but see below for an example response.

I had never seen such a sight as when I first saw the Danes, and their ships. A snarling dragon emerged from the mist to meet us, and was soon joined by a band of axe-wielding savages, with fire in their eyes. They arrived so suddenly, and so silently, that no one knew how to react...not that they had time to. Indeed, this was when I first saw the Danes, but how I wish it were the last.

HOW ARE YOU GETTING ON?

VIKINGS IN
BRITAIN

VIKINGS IN BRITAIN

As we have touched upon, the Vikings were famous for their voyages abroad, which were mainly targeted at Britain and Ireland. While these were often aggressive and violent, there were many Viking visits where stealing and killing were not top priorities. For example, there were a lot of Vikings who came to barter and trade with the Anglo-Saxons in Britain.

That being said, Vikings were eventually able to take over and control a large amount of British land for themselves! In this chapter, we will look at the first Viking visits to Britain, and talk about whether their savage reputation is fully deserved.

Join our English Thane, Aldwyn, as we discuss the Vikings' dealings with the British Isles!

Before we get into the specifics about this topic, let's look at the Vikings' modern reputation.

EXAGGERATED REPUTATION?

Today, the opinion that most people have of Vikings is that they were a band of lawless barbarians, who did nothing but pillage and steal. However, as we have already mentioned, this is too simple a view of their actions. While money was mostly the motivation for Vikings to leave Scandinavia, they did not always murder to get it!

Also, as we have already seen, the Vikings were becoming more and more civilised at home, just as the Anglo-Saxons were in Britain. While violence was present in Norse communities (as we looked at on page 33), they had laws, governments, and codes of honour, as well as a proud culture of art and craftsmanship.

WHY DO WE THINK OF THE VIKINGS IN THIS WAY?

Historians have talked about whether we have been passed on a one-sided or exaggerated image of the Vikings from early Anglo-Saxon accounts. The fact that the Vikings and the Anglo-Saxons had very different religions during this time is very relevant here.

Some of the first Viking raids in Britain were carried out on Christian monasteries, which was very shocking to Anglo-Saxons – an attack on monks was like an attack on God. This could be why the Vikings were portrayed in a devil-like light from storytellers and writers of the time, and why the activity of the peaceful Vikings being ignored.

THAT BEING SAID...

Despite this potential exaggeration, the Vikings undoubtedly had a ruthless and violent side to them. As we have already looked at, they often settled personal disputes through fighting. Also, Viking soldiers' most treasured belief was that it was of vital importance to die a hero's death in battle. These facts also help to create the image of the Viking as a ruthless and plundering warrior.

IN CONCLUSION

There is a lot of historical debate over how we should view the Vikings. As a result, we do not have a clear-cut 'yes or no' answer to a question like: "Were the Vikings a force for evil?"

It is up to you to look at **evidence** and make your own decision!

QUESTION 1

Using the blank table below, write down some features of Viking society that fit into the categories 'things to admire about the Vikings' and 'things not to admire about the Vikings'.

THINGS TO ADMIRE ABOUT THE VIKINGS	THINGS NOT TO ADMIRE ABOUT THE VIKINGS

QUESTION 2

Why did the Vikings not care about insulting the Christian god?

_____

_____

_____

_____

QUESTION 3

Draw your own image of a Norseman, highlighting what you think to be the most important characteristics of a typical Viking. You can choose whether you want to focus on his ability to fight, his craftsmanship, or something else.

ANSWERS

QUESTION 1

THINGS TO ADMIRE ABOUT THE VIKINGS	THINGS NOT TO ADMIRE ABOUT THE VIKINGS
EXCELLENT CRAFTSMANSHIP	MURDERED MANY INNOCENTS
ADVANCED LEGAL SYSTEM	STOLE MANY VALUABLES
DESIRE TO PEACEFULLY SETTLE AND TRADE	TOOK LAND AND SLAVES BY FORCE

QUESTION 2

The Vikings did not care about insulting the Christian god, because they were not Christians. At this time, they were pagans who believed in many different gods.

QUESTION 3

Show someone your drawing! Did they like it?

HOW ARE YOU GETTING ON?

WHO WERE THE ANGLO-SAXONS?

Before we look specifically at Viking raids, let's look at who they were raiding! It's important to know about who the Anglo-Saxons were, and what their society was like at the time of the first Viking invasion. This was around the year 790 (about 1,200 years ago). But first, some early Anglo-Saxon history…

THE EARLY ANGLO-SAXONS

The Anglo-Saxons were originally a tribe that can be traced to Western Europe, about where the Netherlands and Germany are now. Before the Vikings, they carried out raids on the British coast, and eventually became the dominant tribe on the island. Essentially, at the time the Vikings started raiding, Britain belonged to the Anglo-Saxons.

Look at all the similarities between the Anglo-Saxons and the Vikings!

In many ways, the Vikings and Anglo Saxons had much in common. They were good fighters, good farmers, and lived in large wooden houses in families. Families would own enough land to be able to grow and rear their own food, and live alongside each other in villages.

However, rich Anglo-Saxons were able to have bigger houses, own more land, and wield more power in settlements and villages. Eventually, the most powerful men in these settlements declared themselves as kings, turning the settlements into kingdoms. More often than not, the king was the best fighter in the area, as this was how he earned the kingship. However, a king would face frequent threats to his authority, sometimes having to fight challengers for power.

Early Anglo-Saxon villages would also be home to a class of people called Thanes *(THAYNZ)*. Thanes owned more land than most, had bigger houses and were generally richer. Similarly to how the kings gained power, people generally became Thanes due to the fact that they could fight.

Kings would have favourite Thanes who made up personal armies for them. As you'll discover in the next section, loyalty was extremely important for Anglo-Saxons. In any case, it was a good idea to have loyal fighters, as local kings would often fight with each other over land and wealth.

ANGLO-SAXON SOLDIERS

Like the Vikings, Anglo-Saxon soldiers had simple but effective battle equipment. Weapons were light but powerful, and protection was fairly limited. Look at the picture below to see what they looked like.

Only the richest and most powerful Anglo-Saxons could afford to have iron longswords. As a result, swords were a status symbol of the upper classes and the best fighters. The wealthy often decorated their swords, coating the handles with gold or studding them with jewels.

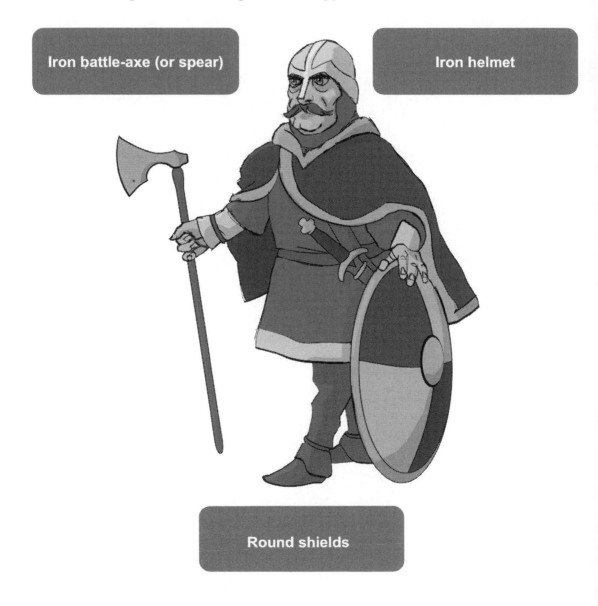

Iron battle-axe (or spear)

Iron helmet

Round shields

ANGLO-SAXON CULTURE

As you will have noticed, there were many aspects of their everyday lives that the Anglo-Saxons shared with their Viking invaders. Similarities can also be seen between the two people's cultures. In other words, the Anglo-Saxons and Vikings had comparable views on spending free time and art. A simple example of this is the fact that the Anglo-Saxons were master craftsmen – like the Vikings. We know this, as we have found buried treasure from this time period.

A very important similarity between the Anglo-Saxons and the Vikings has to do with their attitude to war. We have seen how passionate Vikings felt about fighting bravely in battle – the Anglo-Saxons also believed that it was incredibly important to give their all for their leader. This concept of loyalty between soldiers and their leaders was vital for an Anglo-Saxon; they had a near-sacred bond. Breaking such a bond by betraying a leader, or even showing cowardice in battle, was about the worst thing an Anglo-Saxon could do. Furthermore, Anglo-Saxon kings would have favourite Thanes, on whom they would bestow gifts and land, by way of thanking them for their loyalty.

This sense of hierarchy (everyone having a rank and a place) was very important in Anglo-Saxon society. For example, as in Viking society, women were expected to carry out the will of the men. This meant that they had to do the bulk of the household tasks. Also like the Vikings, Anglo-Saxon men would farm and hunt using dogs and spears. Yet another similarity is the fact that violence would form part of the Anglo-Saxon justice system – disputes were often settled with fights. Men would also fight for their king in campaigns against other kings.

As for what free time they had, Anglo-Saxon soldiers loved drinking mead and feasting together in large halls. Here, they would be entertained by poets and bards, who often spoke and sang of great battles, warriors and leaders of the past. To be immortalised in song like this was a great honour, and would have been something that leaders of the time had in mind and perhaps even aimed for.

The Anglo-Saxons also wrote down their tales and stories; Anglo-Saxon literature (writing) was some of the first to come out of Britain. We can point to great works such as Beowulf *(BAY-O-WOLF)*, an epic poem (written between the years 700-900) as a surviving classic from this era. People still read and enjoy this story today – it was even made into a Hollywood film.

One of the most important and informative examples of this Anglo-Saxon written tradition is the Anglo-Saxon Chronicle.

THE ANGLO-SAXON CHRONICLE

The Anglo-Saxon Chronicle is a huge document, written over hundreds of years by several Anglo-Saxon historians in order to record the events of their time. First ordered by Alfred the Great (see page 77 for more), it represents a hugely valuable historical source that has provided us with huge amounts of information about what England was like between the years 890 and 1150.

The Anglo-Saxon Chronicle is the main reason we know so much about when certain kings lived or where battles took place!

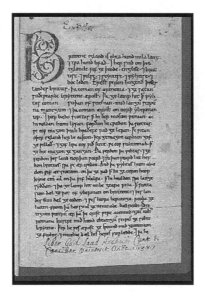

ANGLO-SAXON GOLD!

Over the years, archaeologists have found lots of evidence of how the Anglo-Saxons lived their lives. The treasures that they buried give us an insight into what they owned and what importance their possessions had.

One of the best archaeological finds in British history occurred at Sutton Hoo, Suffolk, in 1939.

THE SUTTON HOO BURIAL

Archaeologists were drawn to undisturbed Anglo-Saxon burial mounds that were located near a river in Sutton Hoo. They began to explore the largest one, and were amazed at what they discovered.

They found the remains of a huge Viking longship, which was filled with untold treasures and riches. For example, there was an iron sword complete with a gold handle, a battle shield, and many bowls made of bronze and silver. Not only that, but buried beneath the mound was an ornate purse filled with gold coins and an extremely valuable golden belt buckle.

However, the highlight of this incredible find was a beautifully decorated and detailed iron helmet.

The investigators soon confirmed that it was an Anglo-Saxon grave.

What do these items tell us about the owner?

CONCLUSIONS WE CAN MAKE ABOUT WHO WAS BURIED HERE

- The sword shows us the grave belonged to a great warrior – they were a very important symbol of leadership for the Anglo-Saxons. Not every soldier was in a position to own one.

- The lavish dining bowls and the massive purse filled with gold show us that the person who was buried here was extremely rich.

- The extravagant iron helmet shows he was a leader. In fact, this grave almost certainly belonged to a king. The helmet was designed to convey power and wealth, with a very masculine design. It even has a moustache!

- The items found in this grave show us the Anglo-Saxon view of the afterlife. Being buried in a boat was said to aid entrance into heaven, being buried with weapons helped them to be better prepared for the afterlife, and the gold was there to help them pay their way in the next life.

ANGLO-SAXON ENGLAND AT THE TIME OF THE VIKINGS

By the time of the first Viking raids in Britain, eight large Anglo-Saxon kingdoms had defeated the rest and had taken charge of England. These were: Northumbria, Mercia, East Anglia, Essex, Wessex, Sussex, Kent, and the Jutes.

These kingdoms were nearly always in conflict – fighting each other for control of people and land. This is one of the main reasons that the Vikings could raid for so long without much trouble; the Anglo-Saxons were not unified or even organised well enough to deal with the Scandinavians in large numbers.

Question Time!

QUESTION 1

Below are three sentences that could be used to describe early Anglo-Saxon settlements. Put a tick (✓) next to the one you think is the **best** description.

Early settlements were ruled by Viking invaders.

Early settlements were ruled by men who were strong in battle.

Early settlements were ruled by Thanes.

QUESTION 2

In the space below, draw your own design for an Anglo-Saxon longsword. Think about decorating the handle!

QUESTION 3

How do you think the fact that soldiers and their leaders had a very close bond helped the Anglo-Saxons in battle?

_____

_____

_____

_____

QUESTION 4

Complete the following crossword:

ACROSS

4. What soldiers liked to drink in the great halls.
5. The location in Suffolk where a huge treasure haul was found.
6. What poets and bards performed to entertain soldiers.
7. If someone was buried with lots of gold, we can tell that they were very

_____

8. An epic Anglo-Saxon poem that is still enjoyed today.

DOWN

1. The Anglo-Saxon _____ is a very important historical source from this time period.
2. Like the Vikings, Anglo-Saxon warriors wanted to die as _____.
3. Some warrior helmets were even decorated with a _____!

QUESTION 5

What can the treasure found in the grave at Sutton Hoo tell us about the importance of the afterlife for Anglo-Saxons?

_____

_____

ANSWERS

QUESTION 1

The sentence that best describes how early Anglo-Saxon settlements were ruled is as follows:

Early settlements were ruled by men who were strong in battle.

QUESTION 2

Show someone your drawing! Did they like it?

QUESTION 3

The fact that Anglo-Saxon leaders had very close bonds with their soldiers would have helped them in battle, as it meant that orders were followed very closely. Also, this meant that soldiers were very committed and even willing to die for their leader. For a leader, these things are very important.

QUESTION 4

ACROSS

4. What soldiers liked to drink in the great halls: **Mead**

5. The location in Suffolk where a huge treasure haul was found: **Sutton Hoo**

6. What poets and bards performed to entertain soldiers: **Songs**

7. If someone was buried with lots of gold, we can tell that they were very **rich**.

8. An epic Anglo-Saxon poem that is still enjoyed today: **Beowulf**

DOWN

1. The Anglo-Saxon **Chronicle** is a very important historical source from this time period.

2. Like the Vikings, Anglo-Saxon warriors wanted to die as **heroes**.

3. Some warrior helmets were even decorated with a **moustache**!

HOW ARE YOU GETTING ON?

FIRST VIKING RAIDS IN BRITAIN

We know that the first raid planned by the Vikings was in the year 793, on the tiny island of Lindisfarne, which is located off the coast of north-east England. Here, the Vikings targeted an undefended monastery, which was packed full of valuables. Vikings will have seen these isolated but impressive buildings and been tempted to pay them a visit.

The coast where Lindisfarne is found

WHAT HAPPENED IN LINDISFARNE?

The raid itself was very one-sided, and over quickly. Vikings sailed up to the coast on which the monastery stood, and quickly overran the whole area. Several monks were murdered; blood was even spilt inside the monastery itself. Other monks were captured and taken back to Scandinavia as slaves.

The Vikings' aim was to get rich from this raid, and they succeeded. Valuable religious items (like crosses and candlesticks) made of gold and silver were all seized. Gold coins, china plates, and ornate books were also stolen by the rampant Vikings. They did not even stop there – the Vikings destroyed half the monastery by burning it down just before leaving.

Unsurprisingly, the Anglo-Saxons were horrified by this attack, the church even said that it had come as a result of the sin in people's lives. The Vikings had scared people in Britain so much that they thought the Vikings represented a punishment from God!

WHAT DID THE VIKINGS DO NEXT?

The Vikings continued to raid coastal areas of Britain and Ireland, and plundered monastery after monastery. As previously mentioned, the Anglo-Saxons did not have an answer to this assault, so people living on the coast were subject to unopposed raids for decades. During this time, Vikings were wary of attacking anywhere far inland, for fear of being outnumbered by Anglo-Saxon soldiers.

The Vikings' plans were simple but effective: arrive in Britain in the spring, take as many valuables as they could carry, and sail home at the end of the summer.

VIKING SETTLERS

However, the Vikings' plans soon changed. Not long after the first Viking raids in Britain came the first Viking settlers in Britain. Norwegian Vikings found the very northern part of Britain to be their ideal choice – this was the closest part of Britain to their own country. We have found remains of an early Viking colony in Orkney, on a small group of islands at the top of the Scotland. During this time, Vikings also settled in Ireland, and parts of Eastern England.

Orkney was a good place to settle because there was free land, warmer weather and good farming soil. They may have needed to fight off some locals but this was certainly not more than they could manage. This would have been worth it because the islands provided a good location for the Vikings to launch raids from – you can look at it like a win-win. At the same time, they had better weather, farmlands, and a shorter distance to travel to find riches!

Soon though, the Vikings priorities changed. The next major wave of Scandinavians wanted to conquer England, not just live there!

QUESTION 1

List three things the Vikings found appealing about the monasteries in Britain:

-
-
-

QUESTION 2

Complete the following wordsearch, which focuses on what the Vikings stole during their first raids of Britain!

```
Y C A P D G J T N Y C F      GOLD
G H P F L C Y N S V A R      SILVER
S B V Q O X E P A N N L      COINS
J W Y F G E S L R S D G      PLATES
H C X W Z X N A O U L H      BOOKS
Z R C T S Z F T O U E I      CROSSES
B O O A H N X E P U S V      CANDLESTICKS
S S I E R X V S H C T T
K S N S I L V E R Q I M
O E S E Z M W O V F C F
O S Q E V Z L V J L K H
B U M B I M V Z I A S C
```

QUESTION 3

Write a little bit about what you think motivated the first Viking settlers to move to England. In other words, why do you think that the Vikings wanted to live in England?

_____

_____

_____

ANSWERS

QUESTION 1

Three things the Vikings found appealing about the monasteries:

- They were undefended;

- They were isolated (far from Anglo-Saxon strongholds);

- They were impressive buildings, which suggests there were valuables inside.

QUESTION 2

GOLD
SILVER
COINS
PLATES
BOOKS
CROSSES
CANDLESTICKS

QUESTION 3

Your answer should mention the fact that the Vikings wanted to escape the freezing Scandinavian weather, gain access to the good British farmland, and get closer to the monasteries they wanted to raid.

HOW ARE YOU GETTING ON?

VIKINGS DEFEAT THE ANGLO-SAXONS

By around the year 850, groups of Vikings began their campaigns to take English land. At first, they would attack major Anglo-Saxon strongholds, taking small areas of towns and cities, and stay there over the winter. This was something that they had never done in the past.

Soon, however, they would start taking huge areas of England for their own! So, how did they do it?

THE GREAT HEATHEN ARMY

Around the year 865, a huge Viking army had formed, united by their ambition to conquer England. This represented a huge difference from previous Viking attacks, which were carried out by much smaller, much less organised bands of warriors. As seen in the Anglo-Saxon Chronicle, Britons called this huge force 'the Great Heathen Army'.

The Great Heathen Army began their campaign in East Anglia, and immediately set about defeating the local king. However, violence was not yet needed, because the East Anglians surrendered and offered the invaders land and money. They were scared of the size and viciousness of the newly organised Norsemen!

Do you think the leaders in East Anglia were wise to surrender?

This was a very good start to the invasion for the Great Heathen Army. Without losing men in battle, they had secured a base of operations for the rest of their invasion.

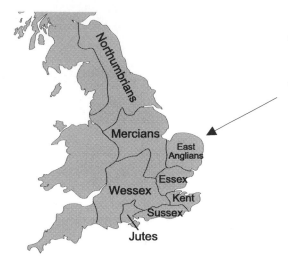

This is where the Great Heathen Army sailed to start their attack – East Anglia

The next place visited by this great horde was Northumbria. This attack went slightly differently to the invasion of East Anglia, as the Northumbrians were going through domestic troubles of their own. They had been fighting amongst themselves, resulting in a tyrant king taking power. This meant that when the Vikings arrived in York – the main city of the Northumbrians – they met a divided force who could not cope with the Norsemen's strength and numbers.

In an attempt to stop the Vikings taking their city, the previously quarrelling Northumbrians eventually joined forces in an attempt to push out the foreign invaders, but they did not act quickly enough. York now belonged to the Vikings, who killed the Northumbrian kings when they tried to take it back.

Viking longships could sail down rivers straight into the heart of major Anglo-Saxon cities – this was very hard to defend against!

The Vikings, now confident in their ability to defeat the Anglo-Saxons in open battle, turned their attention to the kingdom of Mercia. The Mercians tried to bribe the Vikings with gold in exchange for mercy, but they would not find it for very long: the Vikings became known for accepting gold for peace but going to war anyway. So, the Mercian king was soon exiled, and the Vikings were able to consolidate control of the huge areas of land that they had taken.

At this point, there was only one unconquered kingdom in England – that of Wessex and Alfred the Great.

Paying the Vikings for peace was called 'Danegeld', which means 'Danish gold.' It was very unsuccessful!

ALFRED THE GREAT

Alfred, ruler of Wessex, had watched as his fellow Anglo-Saxon kings were defeated one by one. He saw the untrustworthiness and ruthlessness of the Viking invaders, and knew that he had to be smart in order to avoid a similar defeat. His plan to maintain control involved bribing the Vikings as well as fighting them.

Surprisingly, this plan worked for some time, as the Wessexians were able to keep relative peace for a number of years. However, this peace was not to last. A new Viking leader, Guthrum, came to power, and he was not interested in playing nice.

In around the year 878, Guthrum and his men attacked Alfred's kingdom, with the king himself being forced to flee to the West Country to avoid slaughter. This attack was something of a surprise, planned by the Vikings to take place during Christmas. Of course, the Vikings were not celebrating; at this point they still had pagan beliefs.

However, Alfred did not earn the nickname 'The Great' for nothing – he soon rallied his troops and responded. Alfred and his soldiers rode to Edington (located in Wiltshire) to meet Guthrum and his great army. After some very hard fighting, Alfred and his Wessexians emerged victorious. Many Vikings were killed, and those who survived were forced to retreat.

Following this, Alfred actually got the Vikings to agree to a peace deal. This deal even involved Guthrum becoming a Christian. However, the Viking king did not stick to the treaty. The two sides quickly began fighting again.

So, Alfred was forced to modernise and reorganise. For example, he ordered his own version of the longship to be built, assembling a fleet to take on the Vikings at sea. He also built permanent defences, and set up a full-time army that was just for dealing with Viking raids! Fighting continued like this for several years. It was a very dangerous time in England.

Despite this, Alfred was strongly committed to improving the quality of life of his subjects. For example, he was hugely in favour of children having access to education, and took many steps to promote literacy in English, which had been massively disrupted during Viking raids. He also changed the legal system, writing down many official laws that he introduced in England. It is for these reasons, as well as his dealings with the Vikings, that he is loved even up to this day.

Question Time!

QUESTION 1

Imagine you are an Anglo-Saxon city dweller at the time of the Great Heathen Army. Write a bit about how you might feel if you saw this huge Viking force descending on your city.

QUESTION 2

What does it say about the Viking forces that the Anglo-Saxons were willing to give them land and gold to avoid being slaughtered?

QUESTION 3

Draw your own picture of Alfred the Great. Perhaps you could focus on painting him in a heroic light.

QUESTION 4

Imagine you are Alfred the Great trying to raise an army to push the Vikings out of your territory. Write a short speech that you could use to convince soldiers to join and get them motivated for battle.

_____

_____

_____

_____

ANSWERS

QUESTION 1

This answer is based on creativity, but see below for a sample response.

As an Anglo-Saxon city-dweller, you probably would have felt fear if you saw the Great Heathen Army descending on your city. Perhaps you would have heard stories about how it easy it was for the Vikings to take other cities, or about how many Anglo-Saxons they have killed. Also, you would be scared at what people who did not share your god would be capable of doing.

QUESTION 2

The fact that the Anglo-Saxons were willing to bribe the Vikings for peace shows what a force the Vikings had become. As a result, by the time the Great Heathen Army had taken a few settlements, they had a fearsome reputation across England. They had shown that they were capable of mass murder and ruthlessness.

QUESTION 3

Show someone your drawing! Did they like it?

QUESTION 4

This answer is based on creativity, but see below for a sample response.

Men! Anglo-Saxons! We are living in testing times. The barbarians from the North threaten to take our country from us, as they already have from the Northumbrians and the East-Anglians. We must stop them. The lives of our children and our children's children are under threat.

But we can save them! If we unite in arms now, and meet the Vikings in open battle, I know we will be victorious. So, join me brothers, and we will take back what is ours!

HOW ARE YOU GETTING ON?

DANELAW

Eventually, a second agreement was made between Alfred the Great of the Anglo-Saxons and Guthrum of the Vikings. Alfred knew that if he wanted to stop the Viking onslaught, he would have to give them lots of land. So, England was divided up into to two kingdoms: Anglo-Saxon England and the Danelaw. As you can see from the map below, Alfred tactically gave the Vikings the bigger share of the land.

This act created an official boundary between the land that the Vikings had taken, and the land that the Anglo-Saxons wanted to hold on to. Key settlements under the control of the Vikings became York, East Anglia, Leicester, Nottingham, Derby, Stamford, and Lincoln. This clear setting of regions was intended to make peace at last.

But it didn't! Fighting and raids across this border were to carry on for many years. You tried, Alfred...

VIKING ENGLAND

So, what was life in the Danelaw like? Look back to the 'Introduction to the Vikings' section which talks about everyday life for Vikings in Scandinavia. Life in the Danelaw was very similar to this, as the Vikings wanted to live as they did at home, but with the better farmland and weather of England. One major difference was that many Vikings married Anglo-Saxon women, who very often did not have a choice in the matter.

WHAT DID THE DANELAW MEAN FOR ENGLAND?

As previously mentioned, life for Vikings (and others) in the Danelaw was remarkably similar to that seen in Scandinavia. This meant that the Old Norse language was spoken there, the Viking legal system was in place, and a general Viking lifestyle was in effect.

This outside presence had a lasting influence on England's future. In the short-term, this meant that the area became more prosperous, thanks to the Vikings' farming technique and trading connections. Slowly, Viking methods of crafting, building, and farming spread across Britain. As a result, over the generations, the Anglo-Saxon and Viking cultures began to blur into one (see page 98 for more.)

The long-term effects of this Scandinavian occupation can still be seen now. For example, many Viking names for British towns and villages are still used today. Modern place names ending in 'thorpe' or 'by' can be traced back to being owned by the Vikings!

Question Time!

QUESTION 1

Why do you think that Alfred let the Vikings take a larger share of the land following the agreement?

_____

_____

_____

QUESTION 2

On the map below, draw a rough line to show how England was split by Guthrum and Alfred's agreement. Label one side 'Anglo-Saxon England' and the other 'the Danelaw'.

QUESTION 3

Were you surprised to learn that the Vikings had such a large effect on England and Britain? Explain why/why not.

_____

_____

_____

ANSWERS

QUESTION 1

Alfred probably let the Vikings take the bigger half of England to leave them as satisfied as possible, while keeping land for himself. Perhaps he thought the risk of Viking attacks would go down if they had more land to begin with.

QUESTION 2

(This can be a very rough line.)

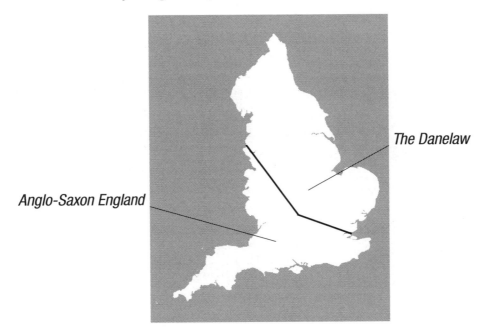

The Danelaw

Anglo-Saxon England

QUESTION 3

This answer is based on personal opinion, but see below for a sample response.

I think it is surprising to learn how large an effect the Vikings had on England and Britain. This is because most people have a fairly simple view of the Vikings. For example, it is easy to think of the Vikings as simply being plunderers and invaders, not as having an important role in developing a culture.

HOW ARE YOU GETTING ON?

THE ANGLO-SAXONS STRIKE BACK

THE ANGLO-SAXONS STRIKE BACK

Inspired by Alfred the Great, the people of England soon got tired of the Vikings owning this huge amount of land. The English were starting to unite as one people, and they wanted their land back. Also, by this point, the Vikings had been living in England for many decades – foreign invaders no longer.

Meanwhile, the Scots were coming together, and didn't much care for the English nor the Vikings. As you can see, all the ingredients were brewing for a huge fight for control of Britain. Who would win?

End of Danelaw

A time of peace?

Athelstan

Spread of Christianity

Alfred was Great, but I am greater!

Athelstan, the first king of England, will guide you through this chapter.

ATHELSTAN

A few decades after the Danelaw was created, Alfred the Great was dead and his grandson had the throne. This new ruler was called Athelstan *(ATH-UHL-STAN)*.

Athelstan's reign is best remembered for his efforts to take back English land from the Vikings, and for effectively bringing about an end to the Danelaw. During this time, people living in England were starting to see themselves as belonging to a wider nation – Alfred arguably invented the concept of 'Englishness'. After the end of the Danelaw, people of Viking descent in Britain would start to identify themselves as English.

Athelstan is one of the first figures in British history whose main priority was uniting the island to become one nation. Of course, he faced lots of opposition, and not only from the Vikings, who wanted to keep control of their own state (the Danelaw). Another group of people standing in Athelstan's way were the Scots.

From around the time of Alfred the Great, people in Scotland had been gradually uniting under King Constantine *(CON-STUN-TEEN)* II (the second). They too had developed nationalist feelings (loyalty to a country), and wanted more land, just as Athelstan did. So, this meant that huge chunks of northern England were wanted by both kings. As if this wasn't bad enough, much of this land belonged to the Vikings, who did not want to give it up!

The only thing that was certain was that the 10th century (between the years 900 and 999) was going to see lots of fighting and death.

From around the year 920 to the year 940, all three forces were involved with fighting each other, with the Vikings often dealing with two attacks at once. With the English attacking them from the south and the Scottish doing so from the north, the Vikings found themselves trapped between the two British kings.

THE ENGLISH TAKE BACK YORK

In the year 927, Athelstan and his troops set about taking back the city of York from the Vikings. This was a daunting task, as York (which the Vikings called Jorvik) was a major city. You can look at it as being like the capital of the Danelaw. However, Athelstan actually managed to take it with relative ease. It is said that he took advantage of the death of the Viking ruler of York to achieve this – they were too weak to attack during this moment of instability.

Of course, this meant that the boundaries between the Danelaw and Anglo-Saxon England were becoming less and less clear. While this was what Athelstan wanted, it created chaos. He also had the Scots to deal with…

ATHELSTAN VS. CONSTANTINE

Up until the year 937, fighting between the English and the Scots had not provided a clear winner. Athelstan and Constantine were both distracted by the Vikings, so both sides were unable to commit to an open battle with their full power.

However, in the year 937, such a battle finally took place. Both kings were able to prepare as well as they could and assemble massive armies. Athelstan convinced many of the historically powerful Anglo-Saxons to join him, while Constantine recruited many Viking leaders to lend a hand.

This gathering of armies had lasting consequences for people in England. For example, Athelstan's success in recruiting many different Anglo-Saxon noblemen led to the English uniting as one. At the same time, Constantine's alliance with the Vikings sped up the process by which they were mixing with people in Britain.

However, this fight was to be extremely bloody, and represented the climax of the feud between the English and the Scots. In other words, it was to decide who would become the most powerful group in England. It was called the battle of Brunanburh.

THE BATTLE OF BRUNANBURH *(BROO-NUHN-BURR)* – 937

While it is impossible to know many of the key events of the battle, we can understand that there was a huge loss of life. The Anglo-Saxon Chronicle calls this battle the greatest slaughter ever seen in Britain. Many important and powerful figures from both sides were killed, but one side did claim victory – Athelstan and the English.

As such, they were able to maintain their control across England, while Constantine was forced to flee back to Scotland. However, the English losses were so great that they did not make as many land gains as they may have wanted.

Following this great battle Athelstan became the most powerful man in Britain. His victory had led many to label him as the first king of a united England.

QUESTION 1

What did Athelstan help create that still exists today in England?

_____

_____

QUESTION 2

Complete the following wordsearch:

```
Z C O N S T A N T I N E O R K          ATHELSTAN
M O J G M P X W G R A Y U I D          ENGLAND
L B Q A S I A G C J T P N G F          SCOTLAND
E R D T C N U E W N I P V B T          CONSTANTINE
Z Y V G O H T L D A O J A Z C          JORVIK
D Z K A T V B D I T N O O F Z          NATIONALISM
P L R D L S F Y P S A R T U J
M M U D A B S Z S L L V U R P
V U I D N U I S K E I I E M B
E I E N D A C R O H S K O A K
P C Q H H J L X P T M Y Q Q Y
T Y L F H U L G P A A Q V L Z
I A G B P D S F N V P E Y D W
P B E R B V R M T E W Q L E J
V C D F Q G H T H I I U A E M
```

QUESTION 3

How do you think the Battle of Brunanburh affected the national feelings of the Scottish and English?

_____

_____

_____

_____

ANSWERS

QUESTION 1

Athelstan helped create 'Englishness' and the sense of national identity that still exists today.

QUESTION 2

ATHELSTAN
ENGLAND
SCOTLAND
CONSTANTINE
JORVIK
NATIONALISM

QUESTION 3

You could say that the Battle of Brunanburh increased national feelings for both the Scottish and the English. The uniting Anglo-Saxons would have shared a common victory, as well as common losses. This battle will have also reinforced the divide between the groups, making their separate identities more important.

HOW ARE YOU GETTING ON?

THE END OF THE DANELAW

As you can tell from the section about Athelstan (page 91), the Vikings were becoming less and less powerful in England. This was partly because they were mixing with the English and Scottish – they were no longer the feared foreign barbarian. Over the decades the Scandinavians had been settling in Britain, the differences between the Vikings and Anglo-Saxons became much less striking.

The Vikings' loss of power is also related to the Anglo-Saxons uniting as one, and becoming stronger as a result. Descendants of Vikings would eventually buy into this notion, and come to identify themselves as 'English'.

All of these ingredients eventually led to the end of the Danelaw. This did not mean that all Vikings and descendants of Vikings left England; rather that the country was no longer split into two kingdoms.

> **Of course, this change was not a peaceful one!**

Fighting continued over the Viking-controlled areas of Northumbria (which they still had after the Battle of Brunanburh) until around the year 954. It was in this year that Eric Bloodaxe, the Viking in power in this area, was killed and the Anglo-Saxons could take full control. After this, the Vikings in England and the Anglo-Saxons began to fully mix with one another.

The death of Eric Bloodaxe spelt the end of the Danelaw, and brought about the clearest image of a united England yet. Although now ruled by one people, England was still a very diverse and often chaotic place to live.

Question Time!

QUESTION 1

Using the bullet points below, write down three reasons that the Danelaw came to an end.

- _____

- _____

- _____

QUESTION 2

In the space below, draw a picture of what you think Eric Bloodaxe would have looked like!

QUESTION 3

Answer the following multiple-choice question by circling **a)**, **b)**, or **c)**.

After the death of Eric Bloodaxe, the group in control of England was…

a) The Scottish

b) The Anglo-Saxon English

c) The Vikings

ANSWERS

QUESTION 1

Reasons the Danelaw came to an end:

- The Vikings had been living in Britain for many years, so they were becoming more and more like the Britons.
- The Anglo-Saxons were uniting as one people beyond the Danelaw.
- Important Viking leaders like Eric Bloodaxe were killed.

QUESTION 2

Show someone your drawing! Did they like it?

QUESTION 3

After the death of Eric Bloodaxe, the group in control of England was...

b) The Anglo-Saxon English

HOW ARE YOU GETTING ON?

SPREAD OF CHRISTIANITY

As discussed previously, the original Viking invaders were pagans – they believed in many gods and were not Christians, as the Anglo-Saxons were. However, by the time the eleventh century came around, this was not the case at all.

As Viking settlers began to mix with the Anglo-Saxons, more and more of them began to open up to Christianity. Some Vikings even seemed to follow both religions! However, by the start of the 10th Century, most Scandinavians (as well as Viking settlers and their descendants in Britain) had converted to Christianity, dropping their pagan beliefs.

HOW DID THIS HAPPEN?

This rise of Christianity was sped up by some important Viking leaders who publicly declared themselves as Christians, and urged their people to do the same. Kings like Harald Bluetooth were responsible for building the earliest symbols of worship to a Christian god in Scandinavia. For example, runestones were created in honour of Jesus.

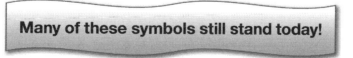

Many of these symbols still stand today!

However, this Christian message was not always shared peacefully. For example, a Viking raider called Olaf Tryggvason *(TRIG-VUH-SUHN)*, who became king of Norway, was responsible for forcing people to convert to Christianity. It was said that he would torture and kill those who refused to call themselves Christians. Of course, this led to a lot of people taking this new faith, as well as many being killed for not giving up their old faith.

QUESTION 1

Complete the following crossword:

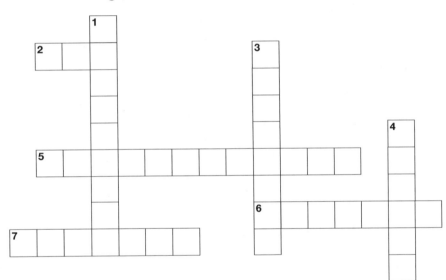

ACROSS

2. Some Vikings followed _____ religions.
5. The religion that the Anglo-Saxons followed at the time of the original Viking raids.
6. Harald Bluetooth built _____ of Christian worship in Scandinavia.
7. The spread of Christianity was helped by many Viking _____ telling their people to become Christians.

DOWN

1. By the start of the 10th Century, many Vikings had _____ to Christianity.
3. The religion of the original Viking invaders.
4. Many who would not become Christians were _____.

QUESTION 2

Why do you think that Christians such as Olaf Tryggvason wanted to kill non-Christians?

_____

_____

_____

_____

ANSWERS

QUESTION 1

ACROSS

2. Some Vikings followed **two** religions.

5. The religion that the Anglo-Saxons followed at the time of the original Viking raids: **Christianity**.

6. Harald Bluetooth built **symbols** of Christian worship in Scandinavia.

7. The spread of Christianity was helped by many Viking **leaders** telling their people to become Christians.

DOWN

1. By the start of the 10th Century, many Vikings had **converted** to Christianity.

3. The religion of the original Viking invaders: **Paganism**.

4. Many who would not become Christians were **killed**.

QUESTION 2

You could argue that leaders like Olaf Tryggvason wanted to kill non-Christians so they could better control the people they were in charge of. Also, such leaders were probably religious fanatics who saw their actions as justified by God.

HOW ARE YOU GETTING ON?

A TIME OF PEACE IN BRITAIN?

As previously mentioned, by the time of the 10th century, the Vikings had been living among the Anglo-Saxons for over one hundred years. This meant that the differences between the Anglo-Saxons and the Vikings began to become less and less important. Vikings were being born in Britain, and a shared national identity was being created. This was sped up by the end of the Danelaw.

Of course, many people in Britain were now children of both Vikings and Anglo-Saxons. This meant that the Vikings and Anglo-Saxons were becoming one people – the English. So, the two groups were becoming one group, and had more and more things in common year on year. For example, they now had the same religion, and near enough the same lifestyles.

All of these factors meant that between the years 960 and 980, Britain saw a time of peace that had very rarely been seen in the past. The king of this time, Edgar, was even nicknamed 'the Peaceable'. During his reign, England became very wealthy, as it focused on trade and development.

Of course, this peace was not to last! A certain group from Scandinavia soon began to raid and invade once more. Was Britain prepared for this?

NEW VIKING RAIDS

While the descendants of the original Viking raiders had apparently settled down, Vikings who still lived in Scandinavia were still raiding and hungry for gold! In around the year 980, new Viking raids on Britain started again. These became much more frequent when the new invaders realised that the English could not handle their attacks.

This series of raids lasted until around the year 1000, and was to lead to a time of unimaginable turmoil in Britain.

Question Time!

QUESTION 1

Why do you think that the fact that England was rich helped the time of peace between the years 960 and 980?

_____

_____

QUESTION 2

Imagine you were a descendent of an original Viking invader, and had been born in Britain. How might you feel about a new set of Viking raids? Think about where your home would be and who you would feel loyalty to.

_____

_____

_____

QUESTION 3

Using the space below to draw a picture of what you think Edgar the Peaceable would have looked like.

ANSWERS

QUESTION 1

The fact that England was rich would have helped because people would have been more able to feed themselves and buy things they needed to survive. This means that people could afford to get along better, as there was less competition for food and supplies.

QUESTION 2

For someone born in Britain with Viking heritage, perhaps the new Viking raids represented a strange time. I imagine that they would feel loyalty to England as it was their home, but would have been aware that their ancestors were once doing what the new raiders were doing. Also, the new raiders did not care who they stole from, Viking ancestry or not.

QUESTION 3

Show someone your drawing! Did they like it?

HOW ARE YOU GETTING ON?

VIKINGS BACK ON TOP

VIKINGS BACK ON TOP

Even though the children of the first Viking raiders were now living peacefully in England, those still living in Scandinavia were still keen to raid and invade! Pretty soon, however, Vikings began to show interest in taking over parts of England for themselves. England struggled to deal with this, so the Vikings became more and more confident. As a result, they began to turn an eye towards the English crown...

Danegeld

A Viking King of England?

Ethelred the Unready

St. Brice's Day Massacre

We're taking over!

Join King Canute as we dive into this chapter!

ETHELRED THE UNREADY

During the time of these new raids in 980, England was being ruled by King Ethelred *(ETH-UHL-RED)*. Ethelred has since been given the nickname 'the Unready', for his famously disastrous dealings with the new Viking invaders.

What went so wrong for him?

Firstly, these new raids were unexpected – England had not had to deal with foreign invasions for several decades. Although there had been lots of fighting on British land during these years, the English were out of practice when it came to defending themselves from sea attacks.

To make it worse, the defences that the Anglo-Saxons had built on their coasts during the first set of Viking raids had not been looked after, and were falling apart. Clearly, England was wholly unprepared to deal with the ruthless Vikings, who were expert raiders at this point.

As a result, many cities and towns across the south coast of England were stripped of their wealth with ease. Ethelred and his armies struggled to deal with this, so the invaders started taking cities for their own. The Vikings wanted to own English land once more.

THE BATTLE OF MALDON

This battle represents the major clash between English and Viking forces at this time. The legend goes that Olaf Tryggvason (who we mentioned on page 103) met the great English warrior Byrhtnoth *(BEERT-UH-NOT)* on the Thames Estuary, with both their armies facing each other off across the water.

The English were greatly outnumbered, but did not back down. So, when fighting started, many English were killed – it was a clear Viking victory. Despite this, Byrhtnoth's bravery in this situation caused him to be remembered as an English hero. We know this because there was an epic poem written about this event, praising Byrhtnoth for his actions. Clearly, courage in the face of death was still something that was very highly respected. See page 59 for a reminder of this idea.

SO, WHAT DID ETHELRED DO NEXT?

Desperate for a solution, Ethelred started doing what so many had done before him – bribe the Vikings for peace. This was a huge mistake – it had never worked in the past!

> The idea of paying Vikings to stop them attacking was called 'Danegeld'.

Question Time!

QUESTION 1

Using the space below, draw a picture of what you think Ethelred the Unready would have looked like.

QUESTION 2

Imagine you are a Viking taking part in this new set of raids on England. Write a short diary entry talking about how unprepared the English were for you! Perhaps you would feel surprised/amused.

QUESTION 3

Why was Byrhtnoth remembered as an English hero even though he was defeated?

_____

_____

_____

_____

ANSWERS

QUESTION 1

Show someone your drawing! Did they like it?

QUESTION 2

This question is based on creative writing, but see below for an example response.

Dear Diary,

Today we sailed to England to begin our new raids there. Even before we hit land, we could see that it was going to be easy! Their pathetic defences were no match for us, and their towns were still filled with gold. We could kill and steal without even trying. Soon there will be nothing left and we will all be rich!

I love England!

Torvald

QUESTION 3

Byrhtnoth was remembered as an English hero, despite his defeat, because he showed extreme courage in the face of death. This was a highly-valued quality for a soldier of the time. Brave warriors would be honoured with poems and songs, while cowardly soldiers would be hated and driven from their homes.

HOW ARE YOU GETTING ON?

DISASTROUS DANEGELD

Ethelred could only watch as more and more of his land and people were taken over by Viking raiders. He wanted a quick solution, and he knew that offering Danegeld was an option. He also would have thought about the fact that England had recently become very rich. All the while, however, he will have known that accepting money had not stopped the Vikings in the past.

Despite everything, Ethelred decided to pay the Vikings the largest offering of Danegeld ever seen in England, hoping that the Vikings would be satisfied and stop attacking. In the end, he paid the invading raiders around a million pounds' worth of silver to go away. They didn't.

Of course, this was an absolute disaster for England and its people. It was an incredible amount of money to offer to an enemy for peace, and it didn't even work! Taxpayers had to contribute to this offering, so people were essentially paying the wages of the soldiers who were killing them.

Ethelred needed a different solution, and he needed it quickly.

Question Time!

QUESTION 1

Answer the following multiple-choice questions by circling **a)**, **b)**, or **c)**.

I.   The fact that Ethelred the Unready offered the Vikings so much money showed that he was:

    a. Confident

    b. Desperate

    c. Smart

II. How was the money raised for this offering of Danegeld?

    a. Taxing the English people

    b. Ethelred's personal wealth

    c. Foreign investment

III. Offering this money was successful.

    a. True

    b. False

    c. Hard to say

ANSWERS

QUESTION 1

I. The fact that Ethelred the Unready offered the Vikings so much money showed that he was:

   b. Desperate

II. How was money raised for this offering of Danegeld?

   a. Taxing the English people

III. Offering this money was successful.

   b. False

HOW ARE YOU GETTING ON?

THE ST. BRICE'S DAY MASSACRE

Following the disastrous Danegeld, Ethelred completely lost control. By this point, he had completely failed to protect his country from the new Viking raiders, and had even paid them for the pleasure of their visit. If he had been desperate before, he was completely panicking now.

In November of the year 1002, Ethelred, King of England, ordered the murder of all Viking men in England, as well as anyone of Viking descent. Many deaths are thought to have occurred during this event, which is called the St. Brice's Day Massacre.

This was a terrible mistake by Ethelred. Not only was it cruel to murder hundreds of innocents, but he had ordered the deaths of his own people by including English dwellers of Viking descent. Many of those killed are believed to be people who were born in England and had shown nothing but loyalty to English rule. This turned many people against him.

Unsurprisingly, Viking leaders in Scandinavia were incredibly angry at this event, and swore revenge. Ethelred had hoped to eliminate the threat of Viking invasions, but in ordering the St. Brice's Day Massacre he made it much worse.

QUESTION 1

Imagine you are an English person with Viking ancestors at the time of the St. Brice's Day Massacre. How would you feel? Think about the fact that you had shown nothing but loyalty to Ethelred.

_____

_____

_____

_____

QUESTION 2

Using the bullet points below, write down two ways Ethelred made his situation worse by ordering the massacre.

• _____

• _____

ANSWERS

QUESTION 1

People of Viking descent living in England would have been disgusted and horrified at the St. Brice's Day Massacre. Of course, they would have also feared for their lives. In addition, they would not have understood why they were punished for the actions of another group – indeed it made little sense.

QUESTION 2

Ways Ethelred made his situation worse by ordering the massacre:

- He turned many of his own people against him by ordering their deaths.
- He angered the native Scandinavians who wanted revenge for the murders of their people.

HOW ARE YOU GETTING ON?

A VIKING KING OF ENGLAND?

The St. Brice's Day Massacre set off a chain of events that would change the face of English history. For Ethelred the Unready, it was going to be a complete disaster.

> **What can you see happening in England at this point?**

Vikings in Scandinavia wanted revenge, and prepared for a huge invasion of England. This would have also been motivated by gold; the Vikings still wanted to make money.

The attack was to be led by Sweyn *(SVEN)* Forkbeard, a powerful king. Sweyn was the son of Harald Bluetooth (mentioned on page 103), so perhaps he was even more motivated than most to fight the English. Legend also has it that Sweyn's sister, a noblewoman called Gunhilde *(GUHN-HILL-DUH)*, was killed in the massacre.

It is thought that another reason that Sweyn invaded at this time was because he wanted to become King of England, and saw a chance to do so with Ethelred in a weak position. In any case, what is certain is that Sweyn Forkbeard was preparing to commit to a large-scale invasion of England.

THE VIKING OFFENSIVE

In the year 1003, only a few months after the St Brice's Day Massacre, Sweyn Forkbeard and his Viking troops landed in Britain. There were several years of raids and fighting between the English and the Vikings, with the Vikings slowly gaining a foothold in England as time went on. The English even started paying more Danegeld!

This war continued for about 10 years. During this time, Ethelred paid Sweyn even more than he had paid the new raiders in the year 980! This had a devastating effect on people's lives as Britain was becoming very poor.

In addition, the people in England were becoming more and more scared and unhappy. As word spread of Viking attacks, people started fleeing their homes; they had no faith that their king was protecting them.

All the while, Sweyn was conquering land and becoming more influential. By the year 1013, he had taken control of many major English cities, and was closing in on London where Ethelred himself was hiding. This was looking like the end of 'the Unready King'.

WHAT HAPPENED NEXT?

The climax of these events was to be rather messy and complicated. In 1013, knowing that Sweyn Forkbeard was closing in on him, Ethelred fled to Normandy in France with his family. His wife, Emma, was the Duke of Normandy's daughter so he knew he would be safe there. Another thing that made him flee was the fact that he had lost the trust of his advisors, as well as the English people as a whole.

This meant that Sweyn could take the kingdom for himself; no one dared oppose him. He had conquered the whole of the country, becoming the first ever Viking king of England. However, his rule was only to last a few weeks, because he died suddenly! It is thought that this was due to illness, but some believe that it was more suspicious than that...

This plunged England into even more chaos. Sweyn's son, Canute (KA-NEWT), was lined up to replace him, but it would not be that simple. News of Sweyn's death reached Ethelred, who saw it as a chance to reclaim power. He returned to England, where the noblemen (who had let Sweyn take power) decided to swear loyalty to Ethelred once again.

Canute, not wanting to risk another long war so soon, conceded and sailed back home to Scandinavia, specifically Denmark. Amazingly, Ethelred found himself ruling England once more, despite the series of errors that had come to define his kingship.

CANUTE COMES BACK

As it turned out, Canute decided to leave England in order to reorganise and build up a new fighting force of his own. So, In the year 1015, he arrived back in Britain with a huge army of Vikings from all over Scandinavia. It was clear that he was not here simply to raid – he wanted the English crown that was once his father's, as well as all the land, glory, and riches that came with it. He was a very strong leader, and came to be nicknamed 'the Great'.

This new war went on for over a year.

Ethelred was about 50 years old at the time of Canute's invasion, and actually died soon after – during the first half of 1016. His son, Edmund, then became leader of the English forces, and king by default. The new King Edmund was nicknamed 'Ironside' due to his incredible ability on the battlefield.

So, the war in England then became a straight fight between Edmund Ironside and Canute the Great for the Kingdom of England. In 1016, a long summer of fighting took place in which Canute was able to take control of most of England, despite Edmund's brave and tough last stand. Despite this defeat, Edmund was able to keep control of parts of the south east of England, on the condition that he did not challenge the Vikings for the rest of the country.

CANUTE AND HIS VIKING EMPIRE

However, the English were not able to keep hold of this last piece of land for very long. Edmund died at the end of 1016, only months after he had become king. It is believed that he was murdered, although (strangely) it probably wasn't Canute who was to blame. As a result, Edmund's death is shrouded in mystery.

In any case, Canute the Great could then take over the last parts of England that were not already his, and become king. He moved to strengthen his position and minimise the chances of any further war or challenge to his power. In a tactical move, Canute even married Ethelred the Unready's widow, Emma (mentioned on page 131), in order to make the people of England more likely to accept him.

His success in achieving this meant that he became a successful and even popular king – he made sure that his reign was peaceful for his subjects. Also, Canute was now ruler of England as well as huge sections of Scandinavia that he already controlled. This is why we can say that he was the leader of a Viking empire.

In the end, Canute ruled for around 20 years, dying in the year 1035. Unfortunately, this event was going to plunge England into chaos once more

Question Time!

QUESTION 1

In the space below, draw a picture of what you think Sweyn Forkbeard would have looked like! Think about his name.

QUESTION 2

Ethelred's dealings with the Vikings had made Britain poor. What else had got worse in this time?

_____

_____

QUESTION 3

Listed below are the events of Canute's invasion of England. But, they are in the wrong order! In the blank boxes provided underneath, write down the events but in the correct order (from first to last).

- Ethelred dies
- Ethelred takes power in England once more
- Canute becomes King of England
- Sweyn dies
- Edmund becomes king
- Edmund dies
- Canute invades England

ANSWERS

QUESTION 1

Show someone your drawing! Did they like it?

QUESTION 2

As well as making people poor, Ethelred's dealings with the Vikings had made people feel unsafe – so much so that they would flee their homes.

QUESTION 3

The correct order of events are:

- Sweyn dies
- Ethelred takes power in England once more
- Canute invades England
- Ethelred dies
- Edmund becomes king
- Edmund dies
- Canute becomes King of England

HOW ARE YOU GETTING ON?

AN ISLAND IN CHAOS

AN ISLAND IN CHAOS

England seemed to be in a state of eternal chaos, with constant battles taking place for control of the throne. Leaders from many different groups all saw themselves deserving to rule England, not just the Vikings. All the while, soldiers were dying in their thousands, while ordinary people had no choice but to focus on their own fight to survive. What a time to be alive…

Who ruled after Canute?

What was life like during this time?

Harald Hardrada

Will the Vikings take England once more?

WHO RULED AFTER CANUTE?

The years following the death of King Canute were complicated, because several people believed that they were the rightful heir to the throne. So, there were many arguments and a lot of fighting over who would rule England. There were four main challengers.

Two of Ethelred the Unready and Emma's sons, Edward and Alfred, believed they had a claim to the throne. They were also competing with Canute and Emma's son, Harthacnut, as well as Canute's son born during his first marriage, Harold.

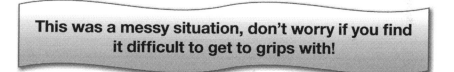

This was a messy situation, don't worry if you find it difficult to get to grips with!

In the end, a few of these challengers ended up taking the throne at one point or another, and none of them did so for very long. Look at the timeline below for a summary of how power changed hands in England between the years 1035 and 1042.

1035 — King Canute dies. **Harold**, Canute's illegitimate son, looks after the throne while **Harthacnut** *(HAR-THE-KA-NEWT)* (son of Canute and Emma) travels to Scandinavia to deal with trouble there.

1036 — While in temporary charge, **Harold** moves to become king on a permanent basis. He is able to rule for four years while his half-brother (**Harthacnut**) is away. During **Harold's** rule, he plots against **Edward** and **Alfred** (sons of Ethelred and Emma). **Alfred dies** as a result of this. Finally, **Harold dies** in 1040.

1040 — After **Harold's** death, **Harthacnut** comes back from Scandinavia with an army, although he is able to take back the English crown without fighting. **Harthacnut** rules for 2 years, until his death in 1042. **Harthacnut is to be the last Viking ruler of England.**

1042 — After **Harthacnut's death**, his half-brother **Edward** (son of Ethelred and Emma) takes the throne. He is to reign until his death in the year 1066, and earn the nickname 'the Confessor' for his religious and peaceful kingship. This represents the start of Norman rule in England – **Edward** had grown up in Normandy (where his mother was from) so he lived a Norman lifestyle and had Norman friends.

Question Time!

QUESTION 1

Complete the following wordsearch about all the people involved in the events leading up to and following King Canute's death.

O	Y	Y	S	S	B	W	A	Z	E
D	Q	S	L	J	E	U	M	T	A
L	M	P	E	R	D	W	U	A	V
O	F	M	T	R	W	N	K	B	M
R	M	U	J	P	A	D	O	V	D
A	A	K	G	C	R	S	P	J	P
H	N	M	E	X	D	M	A	F	B
A	I	D	E	R	F	L	A	I	U
H	A	R	T	H	A	C	N	U	T
Y	O	M	A	E	H	O	H	T	F

CANUTE

HAROLD

HARTHACNUT

EMMA

EDWARD

ALFRED

QUESTION 2

Are you surprised that Harthacnut was the last Viking ruler of England? Think about the impact that the Vikings had on British history up until this point.

_____

_____

_____

_____

ANSWERS

QUESTION 1

CANUTE

HAROLD

HARTHACNUT

EMMA

EDWARD

ALFRED

QUESTION 2

This question is based on personal opinion, but see below for an example response.

I am surprised that the Vikings did not get another invading king into power in England after Harthacnut. They had proven to be an incredibly strong invading force, and had managed to claim lots of power in England over the years.

HOW ARE YOU GETTING ON?

WHAT WAS LIFE LIKE DURING THIS TIME?

So, as you have seen, lots of people from all sorts of backgrounds had wanted to rule England over the years. In the eleventh century, England had seen kings of Anglo-Saxon descent, Viking rulers, and powerful Normans.

In the many wars over England, everyday citizens had lost their lives, and had been forced to pay huge amounts of tax in the process. They had no power over how they wanted their country to be run, and had to focus on their own trades and farming to survive.

Despite this, dying for your leaders in battle was still a vital part of being a soldier, so thousands were happy to lay down their lives in these constant battles for power.

HARALD HARDRADA

After Edward the Confessor died in 1066, there was yet another struggle for power over the English crown. This was because Edward did not have any children, so there was no clear heir to his throne. Three main challengers for the position emerged, all feeling that they deserved it. Unsurprisingly, they were willing to fight for it as well.

Among these challengers was the Viking King of Norway, Harald Hardrada *(HARD-DRAR-DUH)*. Harald had ruled this part of Scandinavia for many years, and was known for his eagerness to invade other areas in order to conquer land for his country. It is said that Harald Hardrada was the last great Viking king whose death marked the end of the Viking Era.

This is because after Harald's death, Viking raids and conquests to foreign lands became much less frequent. In fact, they had basically stopped by the end of the eleventh century. It seems that kings and people in Scandinavia wanted to focus on their own issues at home, and began to stop raiding as a result. This is something that arguably still defines the area today.

HARALD'S ENGLISH CAMPAIGN

So, soon after Edward the Confessor's death, Harald assembled an army and sailed to England, landing at Northumbria in the north east. One of his opponents for the crown, Harold Godwinson (an English nobleman) met him in battle at Stamford Bridge in Yorkshire.

This battle was an extremely brutal one, with around 10,000 people losing their lives in total. However, most of these losses were taken by the Vikings, who were defeated. Harald Hardrada was himself killed, as he was hit in the throat by an arrow. His attempt to become king of England had failed.

WHO BECAME KING?

However, Harold Godwinson would not end the year with the crown either. The third challenger, William the Conqueror of Normandy, would soon defeat the Englishman during the famous Battle of Hastings. He invaded England in the south only days after Harold's battle, so he knew that Harold would not be fully prepared for him. As we know from the Bayeux Tapestry, William was then crowned King of England.

Question Time!

QUESTION 1

Why is the death of Harald Hardrada considered to be the end of the Viking Era?

_____

_____

QUESTION 2

How did Harald help William the Conqueror, although it was not on purpose?

_____

_____

_____

_____

QUESTION 3

Complete the following crossword:

ACROSS

4. Where Stamford Bridge is – the place where Harald and Harold fought.

6. The Viking king who wanted the Confessor's crown.

7. The Norman who ultimately became the King of England.

8. An English nobleman who thought he deserved to rule England.

DOWN

1. The name of the tapestry that shows the events of the Battle of Hastings.

2. The part of North-East England where Harald landed.

3. The part of his body where Harald was hit by an arrow.

5. The king who had no heirs.

ANSWERS

QUESTION 1

The death of Harald Hardrada is said to mark the end of the Viking era because Viking raids abroad slowed down following this event.

QUESTION 2

We can say that Harald accidentally helped William the Conqueror defeat Harold Godwinson, as the Battle of Stamford Bridge provided a huge distraction and led to the deaths of many of Harold's men. William took advantage of the battle to give himself the best chance of defeating Harold at Hastings, which he did.

QUESTION 3

ACROSS

4. Where Stamford Bridge is – the place where Harald and Harold fought: **Yorkshire**

6. The Viking king who wanted the Confessor's crown: **Harald**

7. The Norman who ultimately became the King of England: **William**

8. An English nobleman who thought he deserved to rule England: **Harold**

DOWN

1. The name of the tapestry that shows the events of the Battle of Hastings: **Bayeux**

2. The part of North-East England where Harald landed: **Northumbria**

3. The part of his body where Harald was hit by an arrow: **Throat**

5. The king who had no heirs: **Edward**

HOW ARE YOU GETTING ON?

MOCK TEST

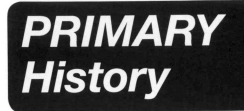

PRIMARY
History

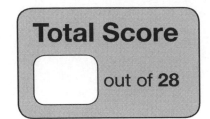

Total Score

out of **28**

Mock Paper:
The Vikings

40 minutes

First Name	
Middle Name/s	
Last Name	
School	
Date of Birth	D D / M M / Y Y Y Y

Answer the following questions about the Viking leader Guthrum, and his dealings with Alfred the Great.

a) In 878, Guthrum and his army attacked Alfred the Great and his men during Christmas. Why did they choose to do it at this time?

_____

_____

1 mark

b) Why did Guthrum agree to make a peace deal with Alfred after the Battle of Edington?

_____

_____

1 mark

c) Name two things that Alfred did to improve life for people in Britain.

I. _____

II. _____

1 mark

 What are the three countries that make up Scandinavia? Fill in the blanks.

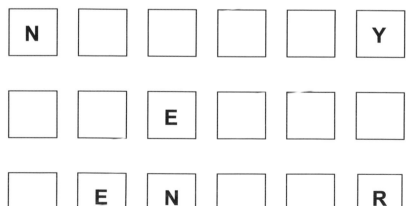

3 marks

3 Name two ways that England's culture and economy were changed by the Danelaw.

- _____
- _____

4 When he became king, who did Canute marry to strengthen his position? How did this marriage help him?

_____

_____

_____

_____

2 marks

5 This picture shows a magical place, special to the early Vikings. What is this place, and how could Vikings get here?

_____

_____

_____

_____

3 marks

Below are three potential definitions of the word 'Danegeld'. Write 'A', 'B', or 'C' in the box underneath to show which one you think is best.

A. Danegeld was the name of the first Viking ship to land on England's shores.

B. Danegeld was the old Viking named for Denmark.

C. Danegeld was the idea of paying Viking raiders to stop them attacking.

 What did the first Viking raiders want to get out of their visits to Britain?

_____

_____

_____

_____

 Why can we say that Harald Bluetooth was an important part of the Vikings becoming Christian? What did he do?

_____

_____

_____

1 marks

3 marks

3 marks

155

Look at the picture of a Viking longship, and label the different parts of it in the boxes provided.

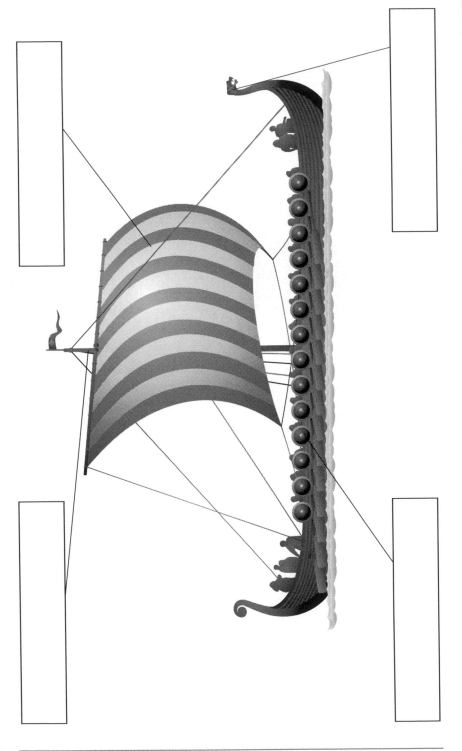

4 marks

10 What was the St. Brice's Day Massacre?

_____

_____

_____

_____

4 marks

ANSWERS

a) Guthrum and his men attacked Alfred and his men during Christmas because he knew they would be celebrating, feasting and drinking. This meant that they would not be expecting an attack. Also, Guthrum was not yet Christian, so he was willing to attack during Christmas.

b) Guthrum agreed a peace deal with Alfred after the Battle of Edington because Guthrum was defeated at this battle.

c) Things Alfred did to improve people's lives in England:

    I. Made the legal system better.
    II. Built schools and made education better.

The countries that make up Scandinavia:

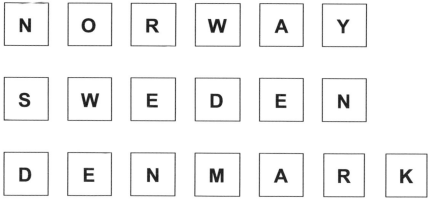

Two ways England's culture and economy were changed by the Danelaw:

• Viking styles of farming were brought into England.

• Viking styles of crafting and decoration were brought into England.

Canute married Ethelred's widow, Emma, in order to strengthen his position. Marrying an English queen would make the English people more likely to accept him. This would also win English people's trust, who took the union as a sign of peace.

The picture shows Valhalla, which was the early Vikings' idea of heaven. Once there, a Viking would spend eternity feasting and drinking in a great hall. In order to get there, an early Viking soldier would have to die bravely in battle for his king or leader. Failure to do so would result in the warrior spending eternity in the early Vikings' idea of hell, Helheim.

The best definition of the word 'Danegeld' is option C: Danegeld was the idea of paying Viking raiders to stop them attacking.

The first Viking raiders of Britain wanted to get money from their attacks. This is why they attacked the wealthy and undefended monasteries first. Soon though, they wanted to take land and settle down in Britain.

Harald Bluetooth was important for the Vikings becoming Christian as he was one of the first powerful Viking leaders to change religion. He also built some of the first symbols of worship to God in Scandinavia.

9

Mast   **Sail**

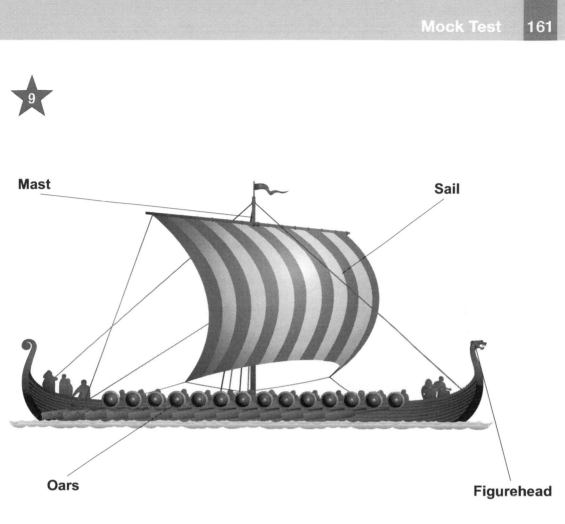

Oars   **Figurehead**

10

The St. Brice's Day Massacre took place on the order of King Ethelred the Unready, with the aim of killing all Vikings and people of Viking descent in England. It was a desperate attempt to bring an end to the new Viking raids on Britain that Ethelred had not been able to deal with. It did not work, and turned many against him, including powerful Viking kings.

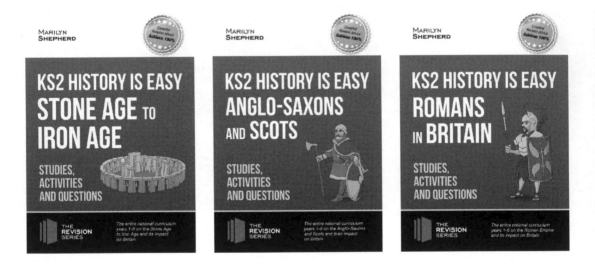

Get Access To
FREE
KS1 and KS2
Tests

www.MyEducationalTests.co.uk

24082270R00093

Printed in Great Britain
by Amazon